May the joy of your Christmas
last all through the year

TO

. . . .

FROM

. . . .

O Christmas Tree

ILLUSTRATED BY

Michael Hague

Henry Holt and Company

NEW YORK

O Christmas Tree,
O Christmas Tree,
Forever green
your branches!

How bright
in summer's sun
they glow,

How warm they shine
in winter's snow.

O Christmas Tree,
O Christmas Tree,
Forever green
your branches!

O Christmas Tree,
O Christmas Tree,
You give us so much
pleasure.

A grove of fir trees
standing near
Brings joy and beauty
through the year.

O Christmas Tree,
O Christmas Tree,
You give us so much
pleasure.

O Christmas Tree,
O Christmas Tree,
Your faith is strong
and steadfast.

It teaches us fidelity
And courage through
adversity.

O Christmas Tree,
O Christmas Tree,
Your faith is strong
and steadfast.

First edition
Published by Henry Holt and Company, Inc.,
115 West 18th Street, New York, New York 10011.
Published simultaneously in Canada by Fitzhenry & Whiteside Limited,
195 Allstate Parkway, Markham, Ontario L3R 4T8.

Library of Congress Cataloging-in-Publication Data
O Christmas tree / illustrated by Michael Hague.
Summary: An illustrated edition of the traditional Christmas carol.
ISBN 0-8050-1538-8
1. Carols—Texts. 2. Christmas music. [1. Carols. 2. Christmas music.]
I. Hague, Michael, ill.
PZ8.3.O15   1991
782.42'1723—dc20   90-25527

Henry Holt books are available at special discounts
for bulk purchases for sales promotions, premiums, fund-raising,
or educational use. Special editions or book excerpts can also
be created to specification.

Designed by Marc Cheshire
Printed in the United States of America
on acid-free paper.
1 3 5 7 9 10 8 6 4 2